AF577777

i was unsinkable

POEMS

SRIJAN ARYA

Copyright © Srijan Arya

All Rights Reserved.

This book has been self-published with all reasonable efforts taken to make the material error-free by the author. No of this book shall be used, reproduced in any manner whatsoever without written permission from the author, except in the case of brief quotations embodied in critical articles and reviews.

The Author of this book is solely responsible and liable for its content including but not limited to the views, representations, descriptions, statements, information, opinions and references ["Content"]. The Content of this book shall not constitute or be construed or deemed to reflect the opinion or expression of the Publisher or Editor. Neither the Publisher nor Editor endorse or approve the Content of this book or guarantee the reliability, accuracy or completeness of the Content published herein and do not make any representations or warranties of any kind, express or implied, including but not limited to the implied warranties of merchantability, fitness for a particular purpose. The Publisher and Editor shall not be liable whatsoever for any errors, omissions, whether such errors or omissions result from negligence, accident, or any other cause or claims for loss or damages of any kind, including without limitation, indirect or consequential loss or damage arising out of use, inability to use, or about the reliability, accuracy or sufficiency of the information contained in this book.

Made with ❤ on the Notion Press Platform
www.notionpress.com

Dedicated to my siblings
and family...

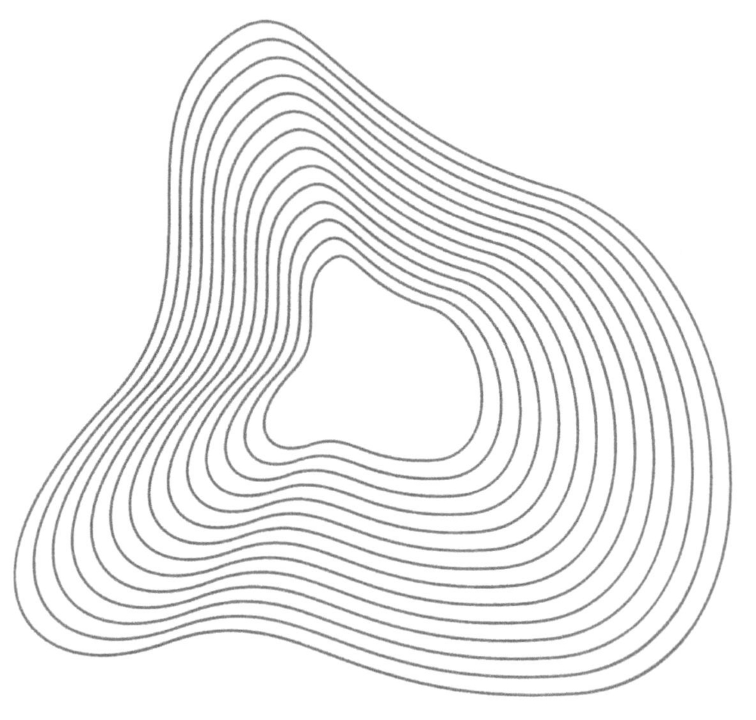

have I ever really existed
or it was unfailingly
living inside me
and now when you are in front
it feels like I am meeting myself

Srijan

ENETTO

About the author

Srijan Arya, the author of this poetry book, is a young writer. With a name that means "creation" in his native language, it's fitting that Srijan has dedicated himself to the art of writing.

A student who has poured his heart and soul into this collection of poems. Despite being new to the world of published works, he displays a maturity and depth of emotion that belies his age.

In his poetry, he explores the themes of love, loss, and the beauty of the natural world. He writes with a sense of raw honesty, using simple but powerful language to convey his imaginations.

lets play hide and seek
come close my eyes
I'm hiding my secrets
now seek for whatever you want

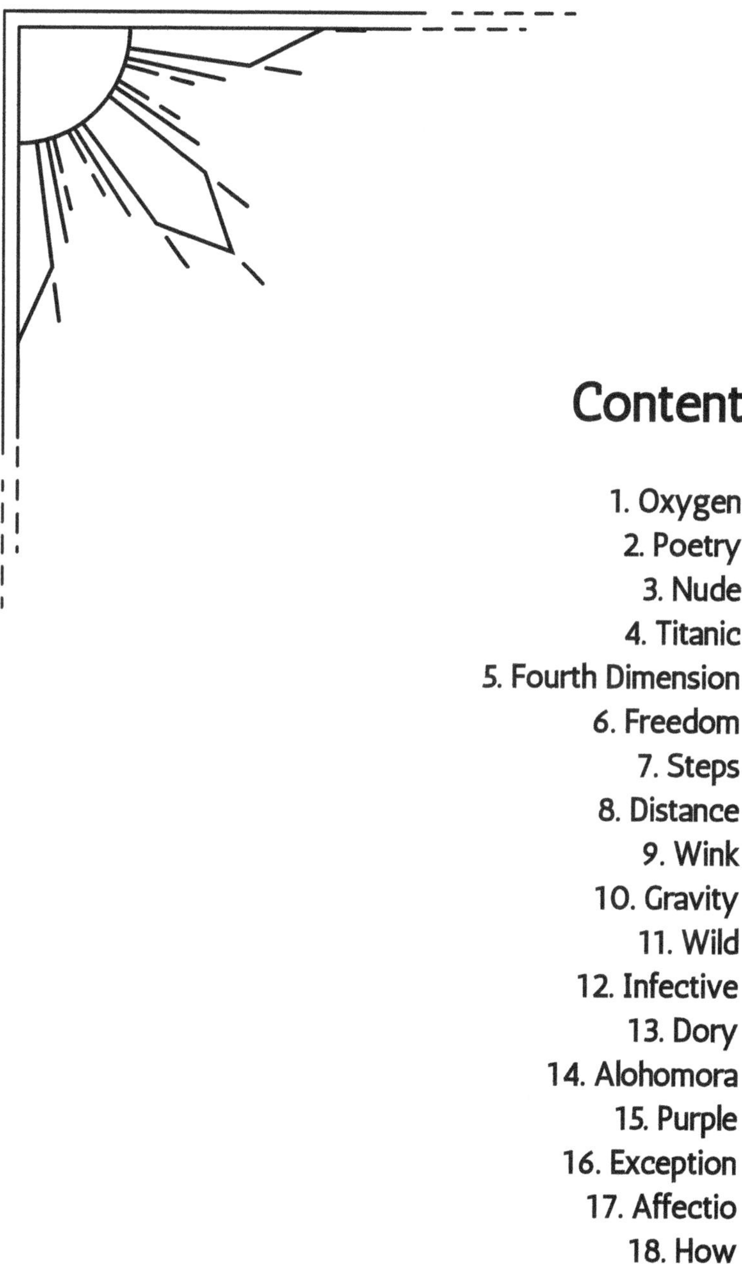

Content

OXYGEN

"sink inside my ocean
lose yourself
let your body
call for help"

OXYGEN

Come to me, hold me tight,
Reveal yourself, let's ignite
Each and every
Drop of desire
From your lips,
A burning fire.
My fingers trace
Your soft, smooth skin,
Discovering places
I've never been.
Don't speak or resist,
I want silence,
Leading to a moment
Of perfect, pure romance.
Love me back and
Melt with me,
As we reach
New heights of ecstasy.
Sink into my ocean,
Lose yourself,
Let your body call for help.
Then I'll come to you,
Breathing new life,
Like the oxygen
You've always needed.

POETRY

"all my poetry
defining her
committed suicide
after acknowledging
she has got
no interest in literature"

Srijan Arya

POETRY

Your body is a poetry,
Each line I read every day,
Your hair like silken strands,
A title to each one they say.
Your ocean-filled eyes,
A cool breeze of couplets true,
Your soft pinkish cheeks,
My lips' prints make them anew.
Your lips, like rose petals,
I still can't tell them apart,
As I make them wet,
They shine like dew on a rose's heart.
Your neck, a bridge of wonder,
Connecting two lands of bliss,
My lips cross it slowly,
Stepping gently so not to miss.
But sometimes I slip,
My teeth catching your skin,
A love-bite in the making,
As I fall deeper within.
Your body is my poetry,
And I read it every day,
With each touch, kiss, and embrace,
I find more words to say.

NUDE

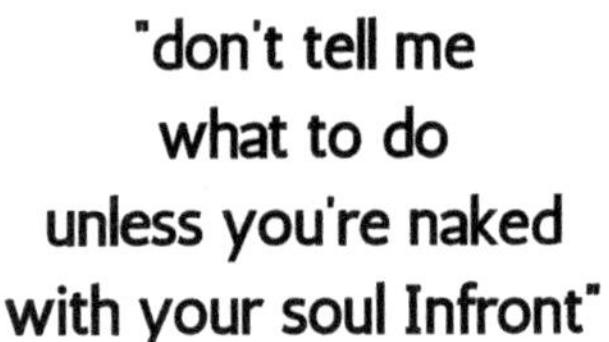

"don't tell me
what to do
unless you're naked
with your soul Infront"

NUDE

I'll always remember that move,
A quick glance he made,
I caught him staring at me,
And when I smiled, he acted crazed.
The feelings were mutual,
We both wanted to express,
I waited for him, maybe he for me,
Our desire we couldn't suppress.
Fuck self-respect, I wanted to see
His face, piece by piece,
Collecting bits of confidence,
To ask for what already belongs to him, at least.
One day he did ask,
And the scenario changed,
He touched and owned my soul,
So tenderly, I didn't feel strange.
He uncovered all my secrets,
That I never knew existed,
Now, even though dressed,
In his eyes, I'm completely naked, no secrets resisted.

TITANIC

"may be i am jack
my sketchbook is filled with beauties
but i am still looking for rose
who can open up her soul to draw"

Srijan Arya

TITANIC

I started my journey
In the Atlantic's deep blue,
Flying on waves,
UNSINKABLE and true.
Against the currents,
Or riding them the same,
I had no fear,
As I carved my name.
But then she struck me,
A cold and icy foe,
And I broke in two,
My fate laid low.
To save myself,
I left no stone unturned,
Some survived,
But many hopes burned.
Why did she do this,
This iceberg of might?
Did I hurt her ego,
By claiming I was UNSINKABLE in sight?
Now I rest on the ocean floor,
Watching as time goes by,
Rusting and tarnished,
With marine life passing by.
But she still floats on the surface,
A smile on her icy face,

Melting slowly but surely,
Her form and presence erased.
Is she water now,
Or is she still the same?
I'm a part of her,
Or is she a part of me, is that not insane?
We fell for each other,
When I was ported on her side,
She hit me not to hurt,
But to make me a part of her, love is so wild.
For love is being a part of her,
And her being a part of me,
An eternal bond on the ocean,
Forever wild and free.

FOURTH DIMENSION

"she is my creation
she lives in
fourth dimension"

FOURTH DIMENSION

Your curves, a gentle arc of a circle,
Hair, akin to the finest brush strokes,
Eyes, black as graphite pencils,
Brows, shaped like precision lead,
Lips, painted with colors as an artist's art,
Neck shadows, blending like tissue shading,
Cleavage, soft as a pastel's hue,
Fingers, like an eraser for imperfections,
Skin, with the texture of canvas,
To me, you're not a girl,
But a painting, in four dimensions,
A perfectly crafted masterpiece,
Of your reality in front of all,
Now and forever, a living art form.

FREEDOM

"finally i saw the moon
that was hiding for years"

FREEDOM

Her image lingers
in my eyes, my thoughts
Her essence permeates
my pencil strokes, my ink blots
Am I a captive
to her beguiling charms
Or is she the beacon
guiding me from harm
I refuse to see myself
as a prisoner, a slave
For in her radiance
I find the freedom I crave
She is the moon
shining in my darkened sky
And in her light
I am forever untied.

STEPS

"eyes deep
hair curl
i danced first
with brown girl"

STEPS

Will you dance with me?
No audience, no judge,
Just you and me,
Close enough to hear
Our breath.
First, we'll hold our hands,
Then metres will reach inches,
Your arm will be
On my shoulder,
And mine will be around your waist.
Some left, some right,
I'll follow your steps,
Some wrong, some right,
And in between,
I'll lift you some height.
Some revolves around my index finger,
And when the track will reach the last stanza,
I'll lay you down on my arms,
Looking straight in your eyes,
Expressing how beautiful you are,
And how beautiful our moment will be.

DISTANCE

"its been so long
my fingers are started
forgetting your touch"

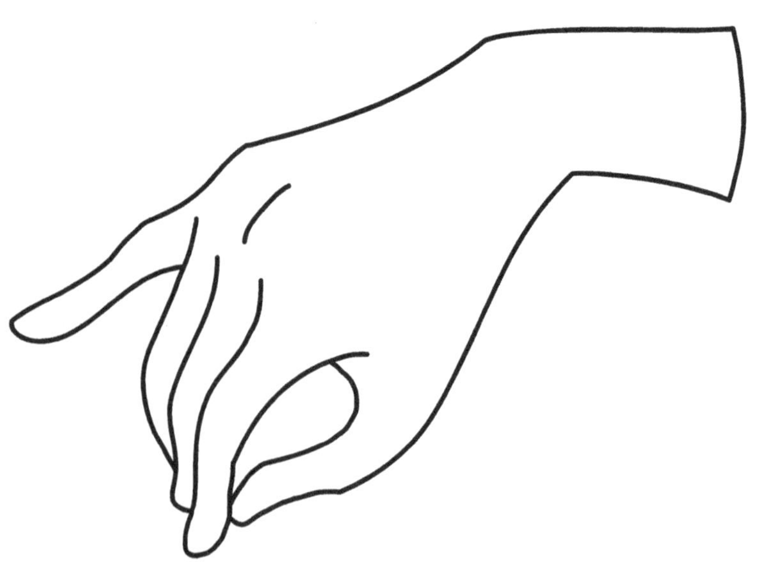

DISTANCE

On first sight,
I didn't fall for those
eyes with their dark depth
or for those lips
that never spoke my name.
It was when my gaze
searched for you
that I truly fell.
The next day,
you foolishly weren't there.
We stood three meters apart
and I couldn't catch your
scent of beauty,
but those lips
left an impression on me.
Now that we're friends
and kilometers apart,
I can still feel the fragrance
of our romance.
People say distance matters,
but to hell with distance!
My soul knows you,
and it can see you and meet you
whenever I close my eyes.
We've never actually met,
but I know you have

a dot under your nose.
No more details needed,
for I prefer not to die
in your hands.

WINK

"eyes talks too"

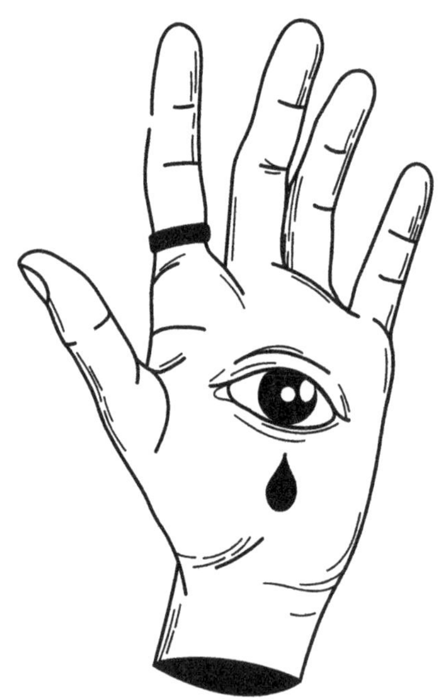

WINK

Not only do her lips speak,
her eyes hold a tale to tell.
The first blink is a greeting,
the second, complex, I can't quell.
Or maybe I use the word "complicated"
to hide the message that her eyes have stated.
The third time she looks away,
Her shyness is evident and clear.
Yes, even her eyes can blush,
zooming in on her iris, I can see the colors appear.
Pupils dilate to capture,
the colors that my eyes express.
Her eyes convey with colors,
what my words cannot address.
The fourth blink holds a pause,
a moment of colorful chatter.
A glance that speaks a thousand words,
bringing our hearts even closer.
The fifth time, she winks,
and I surrender to her charm,
her eyes are a true masterpiece,
and I'm forever under their spell.

GRAVITY

i was unsinkable

"i was lost in space
when your gravity
pulled me"

GRAVITY

I was floating
somewhere in the air
when your gravity
balanced me on the ground
My thoughts were undifferentiated
you gave them a way
I became clear and still
Like a dirty glass of water
that becomes clean when kept on a table
I was lost in the dark
when you crossed holding a candle
and I followed
The best part is
you have no idea you did this
just by showing me
your existence
Your existence
yes, only this thing upgraded me
from typical to antique
And I think it'll work
like magic ahead
To see that magic
you need to stay, girl
Trust me, I won't expect
anything more.

WILD

"she is like cyanide
inhale her and she will eat
your existence"

WILD

She's born with beauty,
the beauty of nature.
I've never seen a flower
using perfume.
She is pure like oxygen,
walking barefoot on weeds,
bathing under the waterfall,
drinking flowing clear water,
and eating fresh fruits from trees.
In short, nature is her family.
If you see her, I'm sure
you'll fall instantly.
You'll follow her,
because she will make you.
She'll be a magnetic situation,
and your veins will get
adrenaline in them.
When she reaches the middle of the forest,
she'll turn to you.
Maybe this will be an amazing moment for you,
but in the next moment she'll hunt you.
Sorry, I forgot to mention that she is wild.

INFECTIVE

i was unsinkable

"she was fire i was ice
she kept melting my existence
i kept erasing her flame
eventually i lost myself
and her as well"

INFECTIVE

Forget those kisses,
mere touches of skin.
Hugs too, like actors perform,
meaningless and thin.
Forget those 'I love you's,
now unworthy of you.
A foreigner has entered,
your system anew.
He reaches the places
where my prints have been,
replacing them with his own,
a malignant scene.
He flows in your blood,
unveiling your secrets,
and some of mine too,
intolerable and egregious.
Therefore, darling, forget me,
forget my secrets too.
You've unlocked my shades of hatred,
for you, it's all I can do.
Yes, I loved and cared for you,
you were a part of me once,
but I've learned to cut off
the infected portions at once.

DORY

"she was bright
i reflected with her
i shined as a star
she left
making me a source of light"

DORY

A part of me isolated,
a part of you isolated,
we became isolated.
Memories are killing me,
I'm not sure about you,
I don't know how he's living inside you,
preparing you to satisfy his hunger.
I'm not sure about your appetite.
I distanced you for a reason,
a reason of love, an unrealized love.
A fish can't choke for oxygen within water,
but my fishbowl lacks its beauty,
colorful stones can't swim like my tiny dory.
Come back into the ocean,
don't hallucinate my signs in him,
wake up and run.
I'm looking, I'm looking,
oh, a miracle,
when I see you coming,
oxygen knocking on my door,
a pure blood with no infectives.
I told you he's a parasite,
your immune system worked on time,
refresh yourself, darling,
I'm getting you an eye-opener

ALOHOMORA

"she casted
imperio"

ALOHOMORA

Her cheeks turned pink
As she stepped onto the classroom platform
To write the right formula on the board
But, oh God, her confidence in writing it wrong
Ignited something inside me, a spark, a kick
I won't dwell on her eyes, hair, and other such things
They have been talked about enough
But I will say this, her eyes are deep enough
To sink into and lose oneself in
The iris filled with dark magic
Capable of besting even Voldemort
And when you said "alohomora"
All the doors to my heart opened wide
Welcoming you, promising you, caring for you
And so much more, etcetera.

PURPLE

i was unsinkable

"i was sunk in blue
hurt an bled
color mixed
and now purple is
what i see"

PURPLE

She sits before me, in purple coat,
Curly hair held by her left hand,
Listening to the physics lecturer,
Teaching the intricacies of wave optics.
Occasionally, she talks with the girl next to her,
Playing with pens or scribbling notes,
But my eyes are fixed on her,
And my pen cannot resist describing her.
She's not mine, but in my thoughts, she is,
A wine un-sipped, but on my lips,
And with each passing moment,
My desire for her only grows.
I know it's not a proper poetry,
Just a mere description of a girl,
But I'm so bored in this lecture,
And she's the most interesting thing in my world.

EXCEPTION

"waiting till you agree"

EXCEPTION

Her name means the ruling goddess,
And no doubt, she rules everyone.
A voice as light as air, a chance to hear,
And when you do, you disappear.
She glows with all her light, she flows with all her grace,
Eyes follow her steps as she walks,
And people love to watch her while she talks.
No makeup, no filter, nothing at all,
Still, she catches the attention of all.
But there is an exception here, and that is me,
I'm not like everyone else, you see.
My eyes are still drawn to curly hair,
Purple coat, beyond compare.
An un-sipped wine,
Meant to be mine.

AFFECTIO

"sipping this coffee
reminds me of you"

AFFECTIO

Your eyes once whispered a secret
When we sat at that cafe
Each sentence began with "we," not "I"
I later learned that "I" meant "ego" in Latin
But you were always selfless
And I wanted to be part of your course
You were a moon, and I was content
Basking in your reflected light
I wanted to shine with you
To be exposed and eclipsed
In the darkest night, you and I
Would bleed the same light
You loved me despite my flaws
Killing me with kindness, healing me with heat
Sealing me in ice, melting and freezing me twice
Until I reached a point
Where my eyes could tell you a secret:
Your name in Latin means Affectio
Honey, it's a clue
To the depths of my love for you.
countless desires of mine
can be fulfilled
with your one smile

HOW

"not touching your reality
my imaginations are enough"

HOW

When we'll meet,
I'll tell you how blessed I feel
to have a part of your existence.
I'll describe how my eyes searched for you,
leaping out of my dreams into reality.
How I've spent whole nights lost in thoughts of you,
my phone screen stained with the imprint of my lips
as it displays your picture.
In my notebooks, your name appears between theories,
my pencil drawing you effortlessly,
unmeasured and free.
It would take a day to recount all the ways
you've captured my heart.
I wonder if you feel the same,
if you have your own "hows" to share.
But I know it's unlikely,
that reality can never match my imagination.
Still, I'll keep playing my part,
cherishing the part of you that I have in my life.

DESIRE

"countless desires of mine
can be fulfilled
with your one smile"

DESIRE

My desire is not
about making you love me back,
you can hate me instead, no problem.
My desire is all
about making you understand.
How I love you,
about it's intensity,
about it's way,
about how I don't hate your dark side,
about how I find you special in this
trillions creature containing universe,
about how I look at you when you're smiling,
about so many more countless 'how's.

UNEXPOSED

"i asked her to kiss my soul
she is still searching"

UNEXPOSED

Last night I wandered in a dream,
A vision of you and me,
We sought each other out it seemed,
I in the ocean, you on the shore, carefree.
It was no surprise for me,
For you are my darling, by my side,
But why were you searching for me?
I'm begging for answers, don't you try to hide.
I was searching for a mermaid,
One who haunts me with her expressions,
A pearl collecting inside my shell, unread,
A fish that should not be in a bowl, in detention.
I sought a ship that was not wrecked,
A sunken vessel that still sails,
All metaphors, a story interject,
Telling of you and all that entails.
You spoke not of my smile or grace,
But of something deeper, a connection true,
You were searching for me in that place,
As I was searching for you, it rang clear and true.
Was it a dream or reality?
I asked, as my heart began to race,
You replied, "In real life, can't you see?
You're my unexposed sweetheart, your beauty I embrace."

THE END

they say
if an artist falls in love
with you
you will never die
now tell me
how do you feel
being eternal

Printed by Libri Plureos GmbH in Hamburg,
Germany